SAMSUNG GALAXY S25

USER GUIDE

The Complete Step by Step User Manual for

Beginners and Seniors to Master the New

Samsung S25, S25 Ultra Device with Tips,

and Tricks

Irwin Stewart

TABLE OF CONTENT

INTRODUCTION..4

• **Why This Guide is for Seniors and Beginners**...7

• **Why Choose the Samsung Galaxy S25**.....10

I. Design and Display............................. 28
Design Changes and Features...........................28
Display Specifications.......................................30
• Display Features..31

II. Performance and Hardware................. 34
• RAM Options..35
• Storage Capacity and Expandability..............36
• Battery Life and Charging Features...............37

III. Cameras and Photography................. 39
• Camera Specifications.................................. 39
• Taking Great Photos Tips...............................41

IV. Software and Features........................44
• Android 13 and One UI 5.1........................... 44
• New Features and Updates............................46

V. Setup and Configuration.......................49
- Step-by-Step Guide to Setting Up the Galaxy S25...49
- Customizing the Galaxy S25..........................52

VI. Tips and Tricks.....................................55
- Advanced Features..55
- Hidden Gems...56
- Troubleshooting Common Issues..................57

CONCLUSION...59

INTRODUCTION

Imagine holding a small, sleek device connecting you to the world, capturing life's precious moments, and entertaining you for hours. This device is the Samsung Galaxy S25, the latest innovation from one of the world's leading technology brands.

The Samsung Galaxy S25 is more than just a smartphone – it's a personal assistant, a camera, a music player, and a gateway to a world of information and entertainment. With its stunning display, powerful processor, and advanced camera system, the Galaxy S25 is designed to make your life easier, more enjoyable, and more connected.

But with so many features and functions packed into one device, it can be overwhelming to learn how to use it. That's where this user guide comes in. Specifically designed for seniors and beginners, this guide will walk you through the basics of using your Samsung Galaxy S25, from setting it up for the first time to exploring its more advanced features.

In the following pages, we'll walk you through the basics of the Samsung Galaxy S25 step-by-step. We'll also provide tips and tricks for getting the most out of your device and troubleshooting advice for when things don't go as planned.

So, let's get started on this journey together! With this user guide, you'll be able to unlock

the full potential of your Samsung Galaxy
S25 and enjoy all its benefits.

• <u>Why This Guide is for Seniors and Beginners</u>

As a senior or beginner looking to unlock the full potential of your Samsung Galaxy S25, This comprehensive user guide is specifically designed for you.

As a senior or beginner, navigating the complex world of smartphones can be overwhelming. With so many features, settings, and apps available, it's easy to feel lost and frustrated.

That's where this guide comes in. Our goal is to provide you with a clear, concise, and easy-to-follow roadmap to mastering your Samsung Galaxy S25.

This guide is perfect for seniors and beginners because:

- We use simple, straightforward language that's easy to understand.
- We break down complex topics into bite-sized chunks, making it easy to follow along.
- We focus on the most important features and functions, so you can get started with your device right away.

Whether you're looking to stay connected with loved ones, capture memories with the camera, or simply stay organized with the calendar, this guide has got you covered.

So, what are you waiting for? Dive in and discover how to unlock the full potential of your Samsung Galaxy S25. We're excited to help you on this journey!

• __Why Choose the Samsung Galaxy S25__

This powerhouse device offers a wide range of benefits that set it apart from other Samsung series and competing smartphones.

• __Unparalleled Performance__

The Galaxy S25 is equipped with a large, powerful battery and a fast charging system, ensuring that you stay connected and productive all day long. Plus, with up to 16GB of RAM and 512GB of internal storage, you'll have plenty of room to store your favorite apps, photos, and videos.

- **<u>Advanced Camera Capabilities</u>**

The Galaxy S25 boasts an impressive quad-camera setup, complete with advanced features like portrait mode, low-light enhancement, and 8K video recording. Whether you're a casual photographer or a serious shutterbug, the Galaxy S25 has the tools you need to capture stunning images and videos.

- <u>Enhanced Security Features</u>

The Galaxy S25 includes advanced security features like facial recognition, fingerprint scanning, and Samsung's proprietary Knox security platform. These features work together to provide an additional layer of protection for your device and your data.

- **<u>Seamless Connectivity</u>**

The Galaxy S25 supports the latest 5G network technology, ensuring fast and reliable connectivity wherever you go. Plus, with Wi-Fi 6 and Bluetooth 5.2, you'll enjoy seamless connectivity to your favorite devices and networks.

- **<u>Intuitive User Interface</u>**

The Galaxy S25 runs on Samsung's intuitive One UI 5.1 operating system, which provides a clean, simple, and easy-to-use interface. Even if you're new to smartphones, you'll find it easy to navigate and customize your device to suit your needs.

- **<u>Why Upgrade to the Galaxy S25?</u>**

So, why should you choose the Samsung Galaxy S25 over other Samsung series or competing smartphones? Here are just a few compelling reasons:

- <u>Latest and Greatest Technology:</u> The Galaxy S25 boasts the latest and greatest technology, including a powerful processor, advanced camera capabilities, and seamless connectivity.
- <u>Unparalleled Performance:</u> With up to 16GB of RAM and 512GB of internal storage, the Galaxy S25 provides unparalleled performance and productivity.
- <u>Advanced Security Features:</u> The Galaxy S25 includes advanced security features like facial recognition, fingerprint scanning, and Samsung's proprietary Knox security platform.
- <u>Seamless Connectivity:</u> The Galaxy S25 supports the latest 5G network technology,

ensuring fast and reliable connectivity wherever you go.

In conclusion, the Samsung Galaxy S25 is an exceptional smartphone that offers a wide range of benefits and features. Whether you're a casual user or a power user, the Galaxy S25 has the tools and capabilities you need to stay connected, productive, and entertained on the go.

Samsung's Galaxy S25 Ultra is expected to perform noticeably better than the Galaxy S24 Ultra.

With only a few days until Samsung's Galaxy Unpacked 2025 event, last-minute reports concerning the company's flagship Galaxy S25 Ultra model—specifically, its upgraded cameras—continue to surface.

Despite the relatively small expected increase in camera hardware requirements, a recent source claims that the Galaxy S25 Ultra would deliver notable improvements in both photography and video.

- ### **High Resolution – Better Video Results, Less Noise**

The report does not specify how Samsung intends to achieve these audiovisual upgrades. However, according to earlier speculations, Qualcomm's new Snapdragon 8 Elite processor and higher-resolution ultra-wide video will improve video quality at night.

4x More Clarity in Macro Mode with an Ultra Wide Camera
This jump is probably due to the previously reported 50-megapixel addition to the Galaxy S25 Ultra's ultra-wide-angle camera. This new sensor's resolution would be four

times more than the 12-megapixel model found in the S24 Ultra.

- **<u>AI-Powered Sound Removal from Video: Audio Eraser.</u>**

This powerful feature, first seen on Google's Pixel 8 series, may soon be available on the Samsung Galaxy line. It seems unlikely that Audio Eraser would be limited to S25-series smartphones, considering the leaker has already provided a screenshot of the feature on a contemporary smartphone. It is expected to be included in One UI7 and was initially leaked on the Chinese microblogging platform Weibo by well-known source Ice Universe.

- **<u>During video recording, seamless camera switching</u>**
The source makes no indication of how the Galaxy S25 Ultra might improve, to some

degree, the smooth camera switching that the Galaxy S24 series currently provides. However, there are several issues with the current implementation. Samsung is most likely planning to use the improved image signal processor in the Snapdragon 8 Elite to improve image quality and smooth the transition between lenses in video recordings.

Along with what appear to be very slight improvements in camera hardware, the Snapdragon 8 Elite will do most of the work to greatly improve AI, features, photo quality, and overall performance for the Galaxy S25 range. Thanks to this improved processing power and Samsung's new One UI 7 firmware, S25 will be an exciting release.

• Unofficial preliminary specifications

Network Technology	GSM / CDMA / HSPA / EVDO / LTE / 5G
2G bands	GSM 850 / 900 / 1800 / 1900 CDMA 800 / 1900 & TD-SCDMA
3G bands	HSDPA 850 / 900 / 1700(AWS) / 1900 / 2100 CDMA2000 1xEV-DO
4G bands	LTE
5G bands	SA/NSA/Sub6 - International SA/NSA/Sub6/m mWave - USA

Speed	HSPA, LTE (up to 7CA), 5G

Announced	Jan 2025
Status	Good

Body

Dimensions	162.8 x 77.6 x 8.2 mm (6.41 x 3.06 x 0.32 in)
Weight	219 g (7.72 oz)
Build	Glass front (Corning Gorilla Armor), glass back (Corning Gorilla Armor), titanium frame (grade 5)
SIM	Nano-SIM + eSIM eSIM + eSIM

Nano-SIM + Nano-SIM + eSIM (max 2 at a time)
IP68 dust/water resistant (up to 1.5m for 30 min)
Stylus (Bluetooth integration, accelerometer, gyro)

Display

Type	Dynamic LTPO AMOLED 2X, 120Hz, HDR10+, 2600 nits (peak)
Size	6.8 inches, 113.5 cm² (~89.8% screen-to-body ratio)
Resolution	1440 x 3120 pixels, 19.5:9 ratio (~505 ppi density)

Protection	Corning Gorilla Armor
	Always-on display

OS	Android 15, up to 7 major Android upgrades, One UI 7
Chipset	Qualcomm SM8750-AB Snapdragon 8 Elite (3 nm)
CPU	Octa-core (2x4.32 GHz Oryon V2 Phoenix L + 6x3.53 GHz Oryon V2 Phoenix M)
GPU	Adreno 830

Memory

Card slot	No

Internal	256GB 12GB RAM, 512GB 16GB RAM, 1TB 16GB RAM UFS 4.0
Main Camera Quad	200 MP, f/1.7, 24mm (wide), 1/1.3", 0.6μm, multi-directional PDAF, OIS 10 MP, f/2.4, 67mm (telephoto), 1/3.52", 1.12μm, PDAF, OIS, 3x optical zoom 50 MP, f/3.4, 111mm (periscope telephoto), 1/2.52", 0.7μm, PDAF, OIS, 5x optical zoom 50 MP, f/2.0, 13mm, 120° (ultrawide), 0.7μm,

	dual pixel PDAF, Super Steady video
Features	Laser AF, LED flash, auto-HDR, panorama
Video	8K@24/30fps, 4K@30/60/120fps , 1080p@30/60/24 ofps, HDR10+, stereo sound rec., gyro-EIS

Selfie Camera

Single	12 MP, f/2.2, 26mm (wide), dual pixel PDAF
Features	HDR, HDR10+
Video	4K@30/60fps, 1080p@30fps

Sound

Loudspeaker	Yes, with stereo speakers
3.5mm jack	No
	32-bit/384kHz audio
	Tuned by AKG

WLAN	Wi-Fi 802.11 a/b/g/n/ac/6e/7, tri-band, Wi-Fi Direct
Bluetooth	5.3, A2DP, LE
Positioning	GPS, GLONASS, BDS, GALILEO, QZSS
NFC	Yes
Radio	No
USB	USB Type-C 3.2, DisplayPort 1.2, OTG

Features

Sensors	Fingerprint (under display, ultrasonic), accelerometer, gyro, proximity, compass, barometer
Messaging	SMS(threaded view), MMS, Email, Push Email, IM
Browser	HTML5
	Samsung DeX, Samsung Wireless DeX (desktop experience support)
	Ultra Wideband (UWB) support
	Circle to Search
Battery	
Type	Li-Ion 5000 mAh

Charging	45W wired, PD3.0, 65% in 30 min
	25W wireless (Qi2/PMA)
	4.5W reverse wireless

Misc

| Colors | Titanium Black, Titanium Blue, Titanium Gray, Titanium Silver |
| Models | SM-S938B, SM-S938B/DS, SM-S938U, SM-S938U1, SM-S938W, SM-S938N, SM-S9380, SM-S938E, SM-S938E/DS |

I. Design and Display

The Samsung Galaxy S25 boasts a sleek and durable design, with several changes and improvements. In this section, we'll delve into the details of the device's design and display specifications.

Design Changes and Features

The Galaxy S25 has a refreshed design language, with a focus on sleekness, durability, and functionality. Some of the design changes and features include:

- New Materials: The Galaxy S25 may feature a new material design, potentially including a more premium glass or metal finish. This could provide a more luxurious feel and improved durability.

- Color Options: The device will be available in a range of colors, potentially including new options such as a deep blue or purple hue. The exact color palette has not been confirmed, but it's likely to include a mix of classic and bold options.

- Improved IP Rating: The Galaxy S25 may feature an improved IP (Ingress Protection) rating, potentially up to IP68 or higher. This would provide enhanced protection against dust and water ingress.

- Redesigned Camera Module: The device's camera module may be redesigned, potentially featuring a more seamless integration with the rear panel. This could provide a more streamlined look and improved durability.

Display Specifications

The Samsung Galaxy S25 has a stunning display, with several specifications and features. Some of the key display specs include:

- _Screen Size:_ The device has a large, 6.8-inch Dynamic AMOLED display. This would provide an immersive viewing experience, perfect for watching videos, browsing the web, and gaming.

- Resolution: The display is to have a Quad HD+ resolution, potentially up to 3200 x 1440 pixels. This would provide crisp, vibrant visuals and an incredibly detailed viewing experience.

- Refresh Rate: The Galaxy S25's display may feature a fast, 120Hz refresh rate. This would provide silky-smooth visuals, perfect for gaming and fast-paced video content.

- HDR Support: The device supports HDR (High Dynamic Range) content, potentially including HDR10+ and HLG (Hybrid Log-Gamma) formats. This would provide enhanced color accuracy, contrast, and overall visual fidelity.

- Biometric Security: The Galaxy S25's display may feature an ultrasonic in-display fingerprint sensor, providing fast, secure biometric authentication.

- *Display Features*

In addition to the display specifications, the Samsung Galaxy S25 may also feature several innovative display technologies and features. Some of the potential display features include:

- Dynamic Tone Mapping: This feature would provide enhanced contrast and color accuracy, by dynamically adjusting the display's tone mapping in real-time.

- Eye Care: The device may feature an eye care mode, designed to reduce blue light emission and provide a more comfortable viewing experience.

- Always-On Display: The Galaxy S25's display may feature an always-on mode, allowing you to view important information such as the time, date, and notifications, even when the device is locked.

The Samsung Galaxy S25's design and display are expected to be truly impressive, with a focus on sleekness, durability, and functionality. The device's display specifications, including a large Dynamic AMOLED display, Quad HD+ resolution, and fast 120Hz refresh rate, would provide an immersive viewing experience and enhanced visual fidelity.

II. Performance and Hardware

The Samsung Galaxy S25 delivers exceptional performance, thanks to its powerful processor, ample RAM, and generous storage capacity. In this section, we'll explore the device's performance and hardware features in detail.

Processor

The Galaxy S25 is to be powered by a large Qualcomm Snapdragon 895 or 2200 chipset. This powerful processor would provide fast and efficient performance, allowing you to enjoy demanding tasks such as gaming, video editing, and multitasking.

- *RAM Options*

The device will be available in several RAM configurations, potentially including:

- 8GB RAM: Suitable for general users who want a smooth and responsive experience.
- 12GB RAM: Ideal for heavy users who want to enjoy demanding tasks such as gaming and video editing.
- 16GB RAM: Perfect for power users who want the ultimate performance and multitasking experience.

- *Storage Capacity and Expandability*

The Galaxy S25 is to be available in several storage configurations, potentially including:

- 128GB: Suitable for general users who want to store their favorite apps, photos, and videos.
- 256GB: Ideal for heavy users who want to store more content, such as movies, TV shows, and games.
- 512GB: Perfect for power users who want to store a large collection of content.

The device may also feature a microSD card slot, allowing you to expand your storage capacity up to 1TB.

- _Battery Life and Charging Features_

The Galaxy S25 has a large, long-lasting battery, potentially up to 5000mAh. This would provide:

- All-day battery life: Enjoy up to a full day of usage, even with heavy use.
- Fast charging: Quickly top up your battery with fast charging support, potentially up to 45W.
- Wireless charging: Conveniently charge your device without the need for cables, using wireless charging technology.

In addition, the device may also feature advanced power-saving features, such as:

- Adaptive battery: The device would learn your usage patterns and adjust its power consumption accordingly.
- Low power mode: Reduce your device's power consumption to extend its battery life.

By combining a powerful processor, ample RAM, and generous storage capacity, the Samsung Galaxy S25 would deliver exceptional performance and a seamless user experience.

III. Cameras and Photography

The Samsung Galaxy S25 has a powerful camera system, designed to help you capture life's precious moments with ease. In this section, we'll explore the device's camera specifications, and features, and provide tips for taking great photos.

- ## *Camera Specifications*

The Galaxy S25's camera system is   to include:

- _Primary Sensor:_ A high-resolution, 108MP primary sensor with a wide-angle lens (potentially f/1.8).

- _Telephoto Lens:_ A 40MP telephoto lens with 3x optical zoom and 30x digital zoom.
- _Ultra-Wide-Angle Lens:_ A 12MP ultra-wide-angle lens with a 120-degree field of view.
- _Front Camera:_ A high-resolution, 40MP front camera with a wide-angle lens (potentially f/2.2).

Camera Features

The Galaxy S25's camera system has:

- _Portrait Mode:_ An advanced portrait mode with an enhanced bokeh effect, allowing you to capture stunning portraits with a professional-like background blur.
- _Night Mode:_ An improved night mode with enhanced noise reduction and detail

preservation, allowing you to capture stunning low-light photos.

- _Super Steady Video:_ An advanced video stabilization feature that allows you to capture smooth and stable videos even in motion.

- _8K Video Recording:_ The ability to record stunning 8K videos at 30fps, providing unparalleled video quality.

• _Taking Great Photos Tips_

Tips for Taking Great Photos with the Galaxy S25

Here are some tips to help you take great photos with the Samsung Galaxy S25:

1. _Use the Right Mode:_ Familiarize yourself with the device's various camera modes, such as portrait, landscape, and

night mode. Use the right mode to capture the best possible photo.

2. _Pay Attention to Lighting:_ Lighting is one of the most critical factors in photography. Natural light is always the best, so try to take photos near a window or outside during the golden hour.

3. _Use the HDR Feature:_ The Galaxy S25's HDR (High Dynamic Range) feature allows you to capture photos with improved contrast and color accuracy. Enable HDR to take your photos to the next level.

4. _Experiment with Angles:_ Don't be afraid to experiment with different angles and perspectives. Get low, climb high, or try a unique vantage point to add some creativity to your photos.

5. _Edit Your Photos:_ The Galaxy S25 comes with a built-in photo editor, allowing

you to enhance and customize your photos. Experiment with different filters, adjustments, and effects to give your photos a personal touch.

By following these tips and familiarizing yourself with the Galaxy S25's camera features, you'll be well on your way to taking stunning photos that will impress your friends and family.

IV. Software and Features

The Samsung Galaxy S25 runs on the latest Android 13 operating system, paired with Samsung's proprietary One UI 5.1 skin. In this section, we'll explore the device's software features, including an overview of Android 13 and One UI 5.1, as well as new features and updates.

- *Android 13 and One UI 5.1*

Android 13 is the latest version of Google's popular mobile operating system. It brings several new features and improvements, including:

- _Improved Privacy and Security:_ Android 13 includes several new privacy and security features, such as enhanced location permissions and improved malware protection.

- _Enhanced Multitasking:_ Android 13 introduces a new multitasking feature called "Taskbar," which allows you to easily switch between apps and access frequently used features.

- _Customizable Interface:_ Android 13 allows you to customize the look and feel of your interface, including the ability to change the theme, icon pack, and font style.

One UI 5.1 is Samsung's proprietary skin, which is designed to provide a unique and intuitive user experience. Some of the key features of One UI 5.1 include:

- _Simplified Interface:_ One UI 5.1 features a simplified interface that is easy to navigate, even for beginners.

- _Enhanced Accessibility Features:_ One UI 5.1 includes several enhanced accessibility features, such as improved screen reader functionality and enhanced keyboard navigation.

- _Improved Performance:_ One UI 5.1 is optimized for performance, providing fast and seamless navigation, even with demanding apps and games.

- ## _New Features and Updates_

The Samsung Galaxy S25 includes several new features and updates, including:

- _Improved Multitasking:_ The Galaxy S25 features an improved multitasking experience, allowing you to easily switch between apps and access frequently used features.

- _Enhanced Security Features:_ The device includes several enhanced security features, such as improved biometric authentication and enhanced malware protection.

- _Advanced Camera Features:_ The Galaxy S25's camera system features several advanced features, including improved portrait mode, enhanced low-light performance, and advanced video recording capabilities.

- _Long-Lasting Battery Life:_ The device features a large, long-lasting battery, providing up to two days of usage on a single charge.

- _Fast Charging and Wireless Charging:_ The Galaxy S25 supports fast charging and wireless charging, allowing you to quickly top up your battery and enjoy convenient, cable-free charging.

By combining the latest Android 13 operating system with Samsung's proprietary One UI 5.1 skin, the Galaxy S25 provides a unique and intuitive user experience that is both powerful and easy to use.

V. Setup and Configuration

Congratulations on purchasing the Samsung Galaxy S25! This chapter will guide you through the process of setting up and configuring your new device. We'll provide step-by-step instructions and valuable tips to help you customize the Galaxy S25 to your preferences.

- *Step-by-Step Guide to Setting Up the Galaxy S25*

Step 1: Unboxing and Physical Setup

1. Carefully unbox your Galaxy S25 and remove the protective film from the screen.

2. Insert the SIM card and SD card (if applicable) into their respective slots.

3. Connect the charger to the device and plug it into a power source.

4. Press and hold the Power button until the device turns on.

Step 2: Initial Setup Wizard

1. Follow the on-screen instructions to select your language and country or region.

2. Choose your Wi-Fi network or connect to a nearby network.

3. Sign in with your Google account or create a new one.

4. Set up a secure lock screen, such as a PIN, pattern, or fingerprint.

5. Enable or disable location services, depending on your preference.

Step 3: Transferring Data from an Old Device

1. If you're upgrading from an old device, use the Smart Switch app to transfer your data.

2. Connect your old device to the Galaxy S25 using a USB-C cable or wirelessly.

3. Follow the on-screen instructions to select the data you want to transfer.

Step 4: Setting Up Additional Features

1. Set up Samsung Pay, Samsung Health, and other features that interest you.

2. Customize your home screen, notification shade, and other interface elements.

3. Explore the Galaxy S25's built-in apps, such as the Camera, Gallery, and Music apps.

- *Customizing the Galaxy S25*

Tips for Customizing the Galaxy S25 to Your Preference

Customizing the Home Screen

1. Long-press on an empty area of the home screen to access the customization options.

2. Add widgets, such as the weather, calendar, or music player, to your home screen.

3. Change the wallpaper, icon pack, or theme to personalize your home screen.

Customizing the Notification Shade

1. Swipe down from the top of the screen to access the notification shade.

2. Customize the notification shade by adding or removing toggles, such as Wi-Fi, Bluetooth, or Do Not Disturb.

3. Change the notification shade's layout, such as the icon size or notification style.

Customizing the Lock Screen

1. Go to Settings > Lock screen to customize the lock screen.

2. Change the lock screen wallpaper, clock style, or notification settings.

3. Enable or disable features like Always-On Display or Face Recognition.

Customizing the Device's Audio

1. Go to Settings > Sounds and Vibration to customize the device's audio.

2. Change the ringtone, notification sound, or alarm sound.

3. Enable or disable features like Dolby Atmos or Adapt Sound.

By following these steps and tips, you'll be able to set up and customize your Samsung Galaxy S25 to your liking.

VI. Tips and Tricks

The Samsung Galaxy S25 is a powerful device with a wide range of features and capabilities. In this chapter, we'll explore some tips and tricks to help you get the most out of your device.

- ## *Advanced Features*

The Galaxy S25 has several advanced features that can enhance your user experience. Here are a few examples:

- _Wireless DeX:_ The Galaxy S25 supports Wireless DeX, which allows you to connect your device to a TV or monitor wirelessly. This feature is perfect for presentations, gaming, or streaming content.

- _Super Fast Charging:_ The Galaxy S25 supports Super Fast Charging, which can charge your device up to 100% in just 30 minutes.

- _IP67 Water and Dust Resistance:_ The Galaxy S25 has an IP67 rating, which means it can withstand being submerged in water up to 1.5 meters for up to 30 minutes.

- ● *Hidden Gems*

The Galaxy S25 has several hidden gems that can enhance your user experience. Here are a few examples:

- _Edge Panels:_ The Galaxy S25 has a feature called Edge Panels, which allows you to access frequently used apps, contacts, and features from the edge of the screen.

- _Secure Folder:_ The Galaxy S25 has a feature called Secure Folder, which allows you to store sensitive files and apps in a secure, encrypted environment.

- _Game Launcher:_ The Galaxy S25 has a feature called Game Launcher, which allows you to access and manage your games in one convenient location.

- _Troubleshooting Common Issues_

Like any device, the Galaxy S25 can experience issues from time to time. Here are some common issues and how to troubleshoot them:

- _Battery Life Issues:_ If you're experiencing battery life issues, try adjusting your screen brightness, turning off unnecessary features, and closing unused apps.

- _Connectivity Issues:_ If you're experiencing connectivity issues, try restarting your device, checking your network settings, and ensuring that you're in range of a Wi-Fi or cellular network.

- _App Crashes:_ If you're experiencing app crashes, try closing and reopening the app, checking for updates, and uninstalling and reinstalling the app.

By following these tips and tricks, you'll be able to get the most out of your Samsung Galaxy S25 and troubleshoot common issues that may arise.

CONCLUSION

Congratulations! You've made it to the end of this comprehensive user guide for the Samsung Galaxy S25. By now, you should have a thorough understanding of your device's features, benefits, and capabilities.

Recap of the Galaxy S25's Key Features and Benefits

The Samsung Galaxy S25 is a powerful and feature-rich device that offers a wide range of benefits, including:

- A large, high-resolution Dynamic AMOLED display
- A powerful Qualcomm Snapdragon 895 or 2200 chipset

- Up to 16GB of RAM and 512GB of internal storage
- A quad-camera setup with advanced features like portrait mode and low-light enhancement
- Long-lasting battery life with fast charging and wireless charging capabilities
- Advanced security features like facial recognition and fingerprint scanning
- IP67 water and dust resistance

Final Tips for Getting the Most Out of Your Device

To get the most out of your Samsung Galaxy S25, here are some final tips:

- Explore the device's settings menu to customize your experience

- Use the Edge Panels feature to access frequently used apps and features
- Take advantage of the device's advanced camera features, like portrait mode and low-light enhancement
- Use the Secure Folder feature to store sensitive files and apps
- Keep your device's software up to date to ensure you have the latest security patches and features

By following these tips and using your Samsung Galaxy S25 to its full potential, you'll be able to enjoy a seamless, intuitive, and highly productive mobile experience.

Thank you for reading this comprehensive user guide for the Samsung Galaxy S25.
I hope you found it informative, helpful, and enjoyable.

www.ingramcontent.com/pod-product-compliance
Lightning Source LLC
LaVergne TN
LVHW051616050326
832903LV00033B/4525